# Broad Autumn

by the same author

# Broad Autumn

Jack Clemo

Eyre Methuen   London

First published in 1975 by Eyre Methuen Ltd
11 New Fetter Lane London EC4P 4EE
Copyright © 1975 by Jack Clemo
Printed in Great Britain by
Whitstable Litho, Straker Brothers Ltd

ISBN    0 413 33780 4 Hardback
        0 413 33790 1 Paperback

The photograph on the front cover is reproduced by courtesy of
W.F. Meadows/Barnaby's Picture Library.

The photograph on the back cover is reproduced by courtesy of
Anthony Common.

## To my wife Ruth

'Love's witness shy
Among my psalming leaves . . . . '

# Acknowledgements

My thanks are due to the Editors of the following publications, in which some of these poems have appeared: *Aquarius, Candelabrum, Cornish Review, Counter Measures, Meridian* and *Workshop New Poetry.* 'Seer and Warrior' was specially written for the Nietzsche centenary issue (1972) of the Victoria University magazine, *The Malahat Review.* 'The Frosted Image' was written in support of the Shelter slum clearance campaign, and was included in the anthology, *The House that Jack Built* (Allen and Unwin, 1973).

The myth of Orual and Psyche, which is woven into the Cornish fabric of 'Porth Beach,' was retold by C.S. Lewis in *Till We Have Faces,* and it is to his version that I am indebted.

J.C.

# Contents

## Broad Autumn

True faith matures without discarding:
All I unearthed, each sky-sign crudely mapped
On the white rasped hills of youth,
Warms me still by rowan-tapped crags
Far up the autumnal mountain,
Incredibly remote in climate, texture, weathering
Of bare stones, from my first insights:
I left no wreckage on those low rasped cones.

There is no snarl of tools
Where broad wisdom calls across the cordial heather,
But the hacked glints my young heart stored
Still tone the subtle comforts and the sharp
Fearful shifts of shade as the blood cools
To admit, and clarify, the expanding mental range.

No pestilence of proud ripeness,
Urbane, agnostic, cankers the wide braes
Which my spirit, eagle-keen now, calls native
In the pale sun's gloss. The spikes of raw praise,
Sparse once on the white hills,
Glow ruddier here against the thinned
Thieving of the schooled foreign crows.

I have not changed my country;
I have grown and explored
In my faith's undivided world.
I discard no primal certainty, no rasped
Sky-sign of the Cross;
But now in broad autumn, feeling a new peace
And the old poise of defence,
I accept the pure trysting lochs,
The full antlers in the glens.

# Wart and Pearl

(To Gerard Manley Hopkins)

White warts everywhere, a land's face never sleek,
Never wholesome, but powerful, looked back at me
As I strained for a ritual, oddly
Like you in my youth: the art streak
Feared fatal, an ego-bulge that blocked
Soul's vows from true bend in the cell
Which should honour Christ's Bride, no pagan Muse.
The grey Body was felt, the midnight knell
Knocked hard on our self-rhythms: we had to choose.

Settings so diverse: cool Oxford halls,
Classic Cherwell, mocked your desert and vortex
As you pitched to and fro, swayed by print and tongue.
I never heard a lecture, except the steam-babble
From engine-house pipes when the squat walls
Vibrated, iron rods and wheels flung
Rasp and boom, explaining haulage,
Pit-peelings dragged out where blasts still vex
The warts' base, the sick slimed rock.

A world you hated — machines, hot boilers,
Smoke-snarl on the brick lip of stacks —
Imaged an awe like that which your cassock
Witnessed to. I found your torn language
Haunt and echo through my desolate hollows,
Between wart-face and grey-lapped beach,
Unreached (since I could not relax
To listen) by a sleek art's singers.
You shared an idiom of blood, heart, mind, all hurt
By divine absolutes — hints that perfection follows
The cell-death, innocence of nest and sap-spurt
Survives, but reels, feels lost to us first in our prone pride.

Your Muse was Jesuit-maimed, but worse maimed
You would have foundered, adrift Wilde's way,
Swinburne's, Arnold's — shades that fell
Akin to your nature's, on the Cherwell. Pagan preen
Kindling limb or canvas or page
Accepts the fated dust, trusts no unseen
Lip at a recalling trumpet —
Lip lodged in Mary's womb
Once for a wart-world's ransom, which you cried
Assurance of in your last Liffey gloom.

If the flesh-ban you bore to Dublin end
No longer galls me, I have not been untrue
To the midnight knell, nor slunk from chastity.
To reject a pagan clue
Brings its apt myth alive in Galilee light
For a few — among poets very few,
But I am one, branching from you at the bend.

Holy and terrible was your single blade,
Grief-glossed for priestly insight;
And your Master, outside Rome's rule, wrung
Such tears from me too. But there followed a ray,
Beyond grey-lapped beach and wart-blight,
Flashing where breast and blown hair mounted
Incredibly on the crest of my vow:
Touched, harboured, balancing now —
Christ-sanctioned Aphrodite.

# Helpston*

I never heard wild geese
Nor sowed wild oats, but the omen
Was there like Clare's, straggling from the fen.
This homeless freak, the artist,
Seems born marsh-magnetised
In some Helpston, between bog and limestone,
Distrusting the hard contours, the creed's release.
Reed-fingered swamp and black peat belt
Make the first rhythms bubble and the frontiers melt.

With moonrise on the weird dykes
Comes an ache of expansion to the soul apart,
So nakedly aware,
Amphibious, sensing illicit freedom
Which the fenced herd dislikes.
Banned fancy ventures with the snail,
Grows webbed in shadow where the frogs croak
And swan's wings, goose wings, beat through mist,
Flying low and spectral, back to a watery nest.

There were fields amid Clare's fens;
Peat-land was turned to wheat-land by skilled drainage;
Dykes rose, blurred daily by farmhouse smoke.
Spring's throb and dreams of harvest,
Soft dreams Clare drew from cowslip and pilewort,
Looked clear of slime, and he sought to enclose
In this delicacy the kissed mouth and foam of hair,
The lover's plea for young breasts held bare.

*John Clare, Northamptonshire's peasant poet, was born at
Helpston in 1793, and was buried there in 1864 after spending
nearly thirty years in an asylum.

Merely instinctive, merely natural,
Unchecked by limestone creed, the greed
Grew: gay love pleaded too often
And a rare beauty was hurt,
Coarsened by tavern stench worse than the bog's.
The white plough-horse trod too deep in the furrows
Of his broken ideal, and his Helpston —
Unlike mine, which choice of limestone saved —
Dropped to the softening water
Till High Beech madhouse hid the crater.

# Seer and Warrior

Raven and Valkyrie haunt the lucid patch
Between the frozen source and the bolt which has fallen
With its tragic point against Christendom,
Against the slave-believers, the humdrum
Pallid traffic of charity.
The ancient pride, an ego straining free
To sever or attach
As the blood dictates, flares again in the north.
A new race must begin, a power come to birth
Like the frowning eye of Odin.

Dark German stage, between Goethe and Hitler,
Bears Nietzsche's calloused hell and loosening brain.
There are wounds enough, most in the fire bearer,
Shrilly questioning as the issue spreads.
What has his will shaped and driven
In fields without a shepherd, forest beds
Without true communion? Seer and Warrior,
He feels a raven's beak, no divine healing hand.
His challenge to cringing cant and sterile pain
Sags to a grimace, immature,
Neither of Christ nor husband.

Before the last breach and raving blizzard
He dreams of rebirth, the grey pagan waters,
Valhalla, or an earth-bride, the nuptial guard;
But both elude him, stirring hatred
That breaks a bough-stump and fastens a thong.
There is barrenness in the distant
Curve of the sea, curve of the woman he needed.
The wind's mastery solves nothing, and the virgin,
Dreading the whip, remains aloof too long.

## Bedruthan

Old steps down the cliff-side yielded, slowly grew
Rotten, so we lounge on the turf,
Thanks to gale's rake and rain-harrow,
Salt spittle the bulging surf threw,
Quick flick and kick of a million sandals,
And heavier boots of coastguards, smugglers long ago.

This is Riviera weather — not exactly
What I call Cornish: I always picked
Power from the grey thrash, the pitted howl.
But the tanning sun's no pledge of safety:
Waters now bland took those steps from us,
And with that news you brought me a feather of a gull.

Picked up on the headland, frayed, with a dusty quill,
That once shared a wing's life, sticking out bare,
It yields stiffly to my finger.
Shed carelessly or in an air battle,
It drifted towards the broken flight,
The paved face that failed: both losses scar the summer.

We lounged unfretted, having a seasoned view
Of short cuts, the inaccessible,
And the dropped plume. Our transcendent track
To warm lavings, our riding halcyon sinew,
Have survived erosion and the snap of mishap:
We smile, sharing what's left, still full beyond the
                                                storm-wrack.

# *Toyohiko Kagawa*

(1888-1960)

Geisha's late love-child, soon orphaned,
Shipped to the rice-fields of Awa,
He was galled by the lumbering treadmill,
Envied the dragonflies' freedom.

He crept to the frog and the silk-worm,
Cried when the light, low and yellow,
Changed the bamboos and the plum shade,
Reached through the slave to the poet.

Gifts for Japan were boarded
In the riddle of Toyohiko,
Tossed from a sleek home's courtesies,
Delicate, tolerant, shameless,

To a raw farm on an island,
Rooms grim with swords and armour,
Where slanting eyes' dull hatred
Matched carved gods in the garden.

Old scrolls and shrouded ritual
Clotted the soil's clear emblems —
Droop of the pallid almond,
Clash of canes in a tempest.

He crossed some subtle borders,
Searched in a mission schoolhouse,
Glimpsed peaks beyond Fujiyama,
A foreign track for his spirit.

Arrows of Christ on the mountains
Dislodged the racial dragon,
Pierced the glossed shield and the idol,
Halted his climb to Nirvana.

In a slum hut he soon knelt writing,
Shaken by cough while a brazier
Burned feebly beside his passion
As mystic, reformer, husband.

Best-seller who starved with the workers,
Plucked poems from prison bruises —
A Bunyan, a Saint Francis,
His big teeth broken in riots,

He plumbed a double mystery,
Found an ascetic cleansing
On the beach where he first held Haru,
In the shack where their children frolicked.

His eyes with their dauntless loving
Became thorn-struck as he grappled,
Fought vice, the twistings of statecraft,
The swollen coils in the churches.

From a rich and illicit birth-bed
He attained, along alley and sea-shore,
Christ's yoke: poor, blind, but married,
Shared heavens unguessed by Buddha.

# Asian Girl in Mid-Cornwall

Temple darkness — oh, send temple darkness,
Vishnu, Siva! Memories should be golden,
Jewelled in soft dusk, my racial stream
Broad and brown, turbulent after monsoons;
But I've been barred and choked by the press
Of hostile climates. I look back
On African heat and steam
Which turned the brown charms black,
Raw and frightening. Now I'm flung to England,
Hard and dry in cold lights: no balm or spices
In these winds that sting the clay-mine dunes.

What's in my blood that this foreign tang
Poisons? The long centuries' beat
Of ritual drums at temple festivals,
When the brown tide lapped low and Siva's fire
Was raised through the girls' bought bodies,
Anointed lotus-buds, wedded to wisdom,
Shielding the snake's fang, the death of desire.
Initiates in the shrine, mystical swoons
In temple darkness . . . oh, how it calls
By contrast with this drab Cornish street!

Silken and lovely behind
The temple towns, green forests teem
With banyan and tamarind,
And wild pineapples lean their pink spikes
Over mountain pools and torrents;
Bright birds and beasts glide and mate,
Vibrant with the temple's secret.

My land waits — jewelled, magical, soft in caress —
While I hear Christian bells, the West's wan mode.
Not a pulse here to reclaim me,
Outcast amid horrors — dead white scabs
On ugly hills, miles of them. I see
Engines with teeth, and evil rays at night
On high cones where men unload
Their clanking monsters; and it's all done
As a life's whole key, untouched by temple rite.

Divanie's light — the proverb in India:
Siva's least-loved wife, served with a glimmer.
But even that seems too painful here
In this grim alien zone.
Send temple darkness — utter temple darkness
Now that the chant of mystery finds no echo,
Now that the machine-world of their West
Reviles my prostration.
Dream-drums, wed me quickly
To some kind god, oblivion.

# In Harlyn Museum

I am back in the eerie room
After nearly half a century's wash and wear —
A survival myself, an exhibit
More vocal than these relics from a tomb.
I feel the ancient air
Thinner now, drawing no menaces
From the intact flints and human splinters.
Outside, in the imitation burial garden,
Slate cists look mellow under the soft boughs.

When I last stood here
My childish eyes were wide, fear-clouded,
Vaguely mocked by the skulls and bones
Lodged in their neat glass cases.
A tide within me groped among stones,
A chilly friction whispered:
'Ancestors, Celts, before Julius Caesar
Sent his legions towards the Tamar.
Something called death, and then,
After a long spell, something dug up
From Harlyn strand.' I preferred it
To ball games and sand-castles on the beach.

Taste for the blanched root,
For morbid candours in an ultimate twilight,
Scarcely stirs on my return; the mature outreach
Is curious but compassionate, holding faith's fruit.
My wife breathes with me in the charnel-house.

We question together, our feet still tingling
From the Atlantic swirl on shingle cleared on graves.
What deities were worshipped

Inside the delicate white curve
Of that girl's skull? Did she tramp inland,
Perform weird rites on the knoll
We call Brown Willy, her dark breasts stripped
In frenzy at full moon?
There where the blank jaw-bones grin
Her lips were wrenched in shrieked incantations
On the moor, in woods and cliff-caves.

They were pressed out for love too, fierce, untrusting,
As the live skull bore the loose veil of her hair
To her captor's face and shoulders.
Bride and mother, tribal whore, priestess —
Whatever her role here in the bay,
Those sockets held a slave's eyes,
Nagged by fire and wave-break on the hut floor.
Often there was bruised, blood-dripping skin
Around those bones. Did her head lie inert
As hunter or fisher slunk away,
Leaving her raped amid furze or seaweed?

Pagan gods, blood-tides groping
Among crumbled stones, flesh hurt
In the unholy lover's hand.
But after Caesar the joyous saints
Prayed where her skeleton lay, a triangle
Of slate at its mouth, in the dumb sand.

Where shall we strike a balance
Between compassion without hope
And a hope so intense
That no compassion is needed?

## Porth Beach

Is it Orual's roll
Or Psyche's bowl I carry, treading barefoot
Back from the outgoing Atlantic tide?
We have passed from loose breaker-bruised sand
To dry tight grain, warm and friendly;
But a myth-pattern chafes and twists
In this Cornish cove, stabbing the holiday
With a foreign and wintry question.

I have just bowed over gleaming breast-high rocks,
Where my love showed me a myriad mussels
Massed on the granite, full of the sea's life,
But closed and reticent in their blue-black shells.

No open voice answers, none relevant
To the myth-frame of my inner journey.
If only the mountain eagle would appear!
If only the kingly bird would cry a decision!
Choughs and gulls alone fly here,
Black or white spies from low cliffs, screeching,
Scanning me with mean local eyes.

I dimly recall the hunt and wounding;
I knew the roar of a landslip, the descent
Into an underworld where I lay almost pulseless
For ten years. But when I struggled back
I brought something strange, unseen, intangible,
A heart-weight of destiny.
I bore it to the altar of wedlock;
I bore it just now to the dripping rock
Where my love showed me the crowded shut shells.

Was it Orual's roll, filled by acid fingers,
Accusing the First Cause? Or did I bring
Back from death's river, in blind trust,
Psyche's level bowl, the unspilt mystery,
The uncompromised surrender?

My love's pressure laps the rigid fear;
Our limbs tingle, drying in the sun:
Soon we shall climb the hill to the field-path.
But even there I shall carry
The unknown token, the question will still tease.

May the judging eagle's verdict
Be merciful to my love:
May the kingly eye see the bowl and the balance
Held daily, the seditious roll
Rotting under the landslip, never my possession.

# Tregargus

A rainbow, like my vesper, arches down
Towards the nibbling waterfall,
And a Cornish valley, enduring its grey doom
Of mundane infiltration, is revived and hooded,
Or crowned rather, with a soft bardic signal.

A stream was diverted so that the pitched grit,
Clay-waste, could crawl and swell on the natural bed,
But the crooked current still arrives and plashes
With a pattering hum over the stubborn boulders,
Hissing a mellowing in the ravine;
And a pipe-line bears the warm, invisible mica
Past scratching hollies in the cleft wood.

Some roofless sheds or clay-dries
Crumble amid trees and small wild fruit
On which poisonous powder, flakes of blown lime,
Preach their wan parable:
This was an evening without issue, husked
Where clammy trenches cut the track dead.

The ravine bends round to a stone-mill:
In boyhood I saw its big wheel flinch,
Stumble down, scrubbed by the pounding trough-torrent,
And the crushed stone was seed-like and sterile
Behind the blind grey wall.

But the soft coloured arch bends, potent now
As my vesper, for grey is refused
At the source of the bardic span
The waterfall's thrum is mesmeric,
Half-sad, yet matching the rainbow, the curve
Of a song diverted, reaching us after the blast.

# The Rift

Always the scuffle on cracking slag
Up and down the rift
Between the champing engine and the laid crag.
Sputter and snatch of prayer-torment,
Amid the tucked black thistles and a blown thorn,
Made the convulsion cosmic, naming the worn
And warring clay-God. All my youth was spent
Fighting there, with no chance to sift
Or study, develop the thinker's gift.

Then a ground-mist from the watching sea
Sucked at the raided mine-cap,
Dulled the splinter of ash, lay softly
As fleece on the darkling rut. I scrambled higher:
No cogs now shook the engine wall,
And above it a calm star confirmed the final
Blotting of rough ransom. Faith and desire
Took the broad heaven's sign, felt the far sea's tap:
I was still, and freed thought filled the gap.

# Testament

(To Joseph Hocking)*

Genesis mixed: your Terras tap on clean tin
Foreign to me, though your birth-bed
Was only a mile from mine, the hacked hills
Around us carried the white scriptures
Of a sullen trade, the black Bibles were pounded
In Wesley's fold to make us akin,
And your family blood reached me, according
   to legal files.

But my craggy and uncouth image
Came another way: Knox-souled and Burns-hearted,
How could I take the sleek service
And the tidy text? My genesis
Was spelled in the scummed saddlebacks
Lolling towards the blasted circle,
The whipped fingers of rock on the pit-floor,
Hoisted hoses making their impress
On rinsed and haggard cliff-faces that wore
Slowly away, starting up at smoke-lidded stacks.

Brute tools broke me in the riding stillness
Of infancy, then the loping waggons,
Glum and fast on the drummed tracks,
Woke me each morning, along with the brayed
Or shrieked summons of engine-house sirens.

*Joseph Hocking (1855-1937), Cornish novelist and Methodist
minister, was a Terras tin-miner's son, a cousin of the present
writer.

My boyhood's dream crossed a mineral stage
Without lark's song or bowing myrtle,
But always with an unbegreyed
Gesture apprehended, God's and woman's
Blood-leap — not in your mild pattern
Of the clean sheet and Victorian climate,
But storming to my unwritten page,
Anguished for all the lost Edens.

Neither the hint of mineral
Iron nail in the Godhead, nor the shuttle
And prick of moon-change in the bride,
Could check the released heart's witness
That nightmares abate, that the scummed scroll
Spells no legacy where the heaven-eyed
Invader draws love beyond the Fall.

My dream drained slowly to the blown tress
And the waking unscourged fingers: wave after wave
Of pleasure would interpret
My opened wealth. So there came to your parish
What old defiant Knox found in Margaret,
What Burns sought with tears at Mary's grave.

# John Wesley

His mother-chained heart
Mother Church chained too:
A double guard.
Against it the Cotswold cuckoo
Tossed a challenge vainly,
And the night sky, spring-starred
Above a Stanton arbour,
Failed to prompt the kiss:
So strong were Epworth's clanking codes
And the rivets of à Kempis.

Saga of retreat
From burning stairs:
The cripple was afraid
Because of family scars.
Lascivious poet-fumes
Licking the iron head;
Sisters' bodies bleeding
After legal rape. . . .
In his Oxford cell, his Holy Club,
The shielding Mother took shape.

Mature and expansive,
The drab shadow drained
Heat from Georgia backwoods,
Where he drilled and strained
For his bony harvest,
Till a camp-fire called the blood's
Spark while a girl lay on grass,
Her log-flushed features pleading,
Leagued with the dark stirring forest. . . .
Cruel then, the pious sting.

Mortified, re-moulded,
Fetters nearly lost
As all Britain caught the glow
Of his crackling Pentecost,
He rode among Lakeland hills
With his soul-bride, and would follow
The ultimate eucharist
Through her body's mating light;
But spectres mocked the pure beauty
With torture-screws and charred flight.

Stumbling, numbly docile,
He soon felt a shrew's tongue
Hiss, her fingers rake him:
Conjugal horrors wrung
A strange warmth, crossing Aldersgate's,
From the resigned system.
Monk-armoured, atrophied,
Grey lonely horseman
Leading a rapturous wedded
Host, he knew the last ban.

His Bethel is closed and sold
Today in the preening village:
House built without thought
Of his poignant pilgrimage —
More poignant than an artist's,
For a grace was brought
Deeper than art probes. The baptism
Of lovers' tears at Stanton,
Savannah, Leeds, lit and softened
His hymn of crucifixion.

# The Harassed Preacher

Now that summer has brimmed on the uplands
   White mine-crusts seed in the sun,
And around each pit and its outcast grit
   A gabble of green is spun.
*Soon silenced by bomb and gun.*

Bushes have bragged into blossom,
   Flicked by the teasing sand;
Milk-wan streams vein the valley's dreams;
   Larks lilt where the tip-beams stand.
*Faith's dream and song are banned.*

Our forefathers dug in the field here,
   Built us a preaching-place,
So that truth might spread from the ringing bed
   Ruled by the Galilee base.
*Too distant now — no trace.*

A hundred summers have panted
   Along our zigzag lanes
Since the first raw crowd of converts bowed
   Inside these window panes.
*But the analyst explains. . . .*

The seats were rough bare benches;
   No organ spun a tune;
The squeaky hymns and unwashed limbs
   Made a meagre mock at June.
*The new age mocks the boon.*

Grains from the towering scriptures
    Were flicked by the winds of prayer:
In our grit-ringed nook those drab lives took
    Fresh shape in Wesley's air.
*Now shapeless atoms wear. . . .*

We toil in a fevered season;
    Soul-crusts lie hard on the hill.
Do our tools ring true? Don't we signal through
    To a ruling Potter still?
*Our super-egos spill. . . .*

A plague on the heckling voices
    That would check my sermon's flight!
It's eleven o'clock and here's my flock —
    Five villagers, old and bright,
Knowing their faith is right.

# A Young Mystic

I. *Goonamarris, 1933.*

All very well for the gregarious Donne
To see mankind as solid, unified,
A mainland knocked by a common tide,
The whole mass robbed when death removed a stone.
But rare souls rise from rock-cells blown
From meteors, falling far out — solitaries,
Twisted spikes that snarl or shine alone.

I am poisonous crag; the thriving block rejects me:
The drill on its streets and mountains, the helm
In trade-brisk harbour and river,
Fulfil no itch or quest resembling mine.
My fellow men? The phrase is meaningless
When every ship that shuffles round my pillar
Bears flag and cargo of an unknown realm.
The upturned face is never of my species;
If any call or sign
Comes through gale or mist, it is foreign:
I bristle and flash and am at war.

I cannot be the norm, the human being
Fretted by fear of bombs or of the sack,
Vivid with friends, agreeing or disagreeing,
Thrilled with pride to see a Union Jack.
For me there is no union
Beyond the primal bonds of God and sex,
And these are so formed in me, so meteor-flaked,
That no-one on the mainland, no-one
On the trading decks, would guess
What I mean by the Name, what I seek in a kiss.

My lot's no part of suffering mankind,
For human ills throb through the whole mass,

Are understood and draw forth sympathy.
I think of the afflicted, deaf or blind
Or crippled: they remain inside
The general strata of human pain,
And their thirst is slaked
By the usual plaudit: they are not lonely
With my aloofness — that of a star-grain.

II. *Goonamarris, 1940.*

What growth could end the quarrel?
    Only the unique Rock
Where the mainland was exposed
    At the crow of a cock,
And in Peter's broken seam
    New love-cells could gleam.

How could love bridge the distance
    To my tongue of stellar pride?
The Source of all cells was there,
    Seeking mine for His Bride.
A church ray struck my base,
    Blessed the misfitting face.

How did I snap the selfhood
    That rasped at Peter's keys?
All fear of the trading craft
    Thawed in singing seas:
The Image that baulked my curse
    Courted the universe.

# A Night in Soho

(To John Donne)

That night in Soho — the only night
I ever spent in London — you
Towered, more awesome than the trite,
Though gracious, plaster saints I scarcely knew.
I had plumbed your weird cavern often, drawn
From my drained Wesleyan cell
Deep in clayscape, to your dark and dawn:
They freed me from my age, which spun the crossed shell
Or the hot phallic image in the neon-swell.

I had skirted bomb rubble, stumbling in
From the street to that Catholic boarding-house:
I felt the medieval terrors — sin,
Judgment and the worms' distilled carouse.
Only St Paul's, your intact stone
Tongue, chimed a post-war grace.
You hymned the whore's licence and the rake's bone,
Then blasted through to our time, to me in that place,
The art of a coping penitence, renewing the race.

I lay in bed, still a young man
Groping for love, and your shade towered
Among my thoughts of Cornwall, Ann,
And the cavern of truth where the new seeds
    flashed and flowered.
I knew I was following you: there were tears
I remembered, on a soft key —
Some dream-form of pure earth on which appears,
As Ann's full ardours showed you constantly,
Christ's Passion-mark, chilling the wit of our vanity.

I was soon whisked back to Paddington:
A city more pagan while I slept
Than when you preached, cried to the sun.
Had I alone shared your contrite gloom and kept
Your ray, with cold saints beside my bed?
Fierce battling sensualist,
For whom the bell tolled in the maidenhead,
And the Lamb's blood, at work in the carnal twist,
Raised the true ecstasy of the soul's alchemist!

# Josephine Butler

These brothel steps lead back to Mersey grime,
Gas-jets and a foul wind fretting the street,
Spidery shadows everywhere.
It's past midnight, the waiting-rooms are packed:
Troops, boys of eighteen. . . . I have been inside,
Spoken to some of them, made contact
With girls tripping out to solicit.
My tears and prayers go burning into the slime,
The web that trails from the blood's tricked heat.
God, why do I dare —
I, married and fifty — defy the established crime?

While a million wives lie free, soothed with their husbands,
Unhaunted by harlots' laughter, in a sweet swell
Like that which cured my unstrung girlhood's
Acid of questions, I am driven to docks and stews,
To the soul's vicarious, bitterest black sands,
Where the urge of rescue receives the bruise
From the stony chattel, the cynical male stride,
The trafficker's manipulation
Of a State licence to buy and sell.
I lead my period's
Christ-war on vice, on a vast betrayal — England's.

I've fought the C.D. Acts and Bruce's Bill,
Morals police, the regulated sewer,
And apathy in decorous pews.
My life was sometimes threatened: brothel-keepers
Worked up the mob, set buildings blazing. Still
I thrust at public conscience, gave lepers
The tender truth, slipping through the official
Cordon of steel-toned disgust
To bid Christ's martyred love conquer.
Fire in me cannot choose:
Pure flame would gut cruel threads,
    snap the last dark thrill.

## Comeley Bank

October wedding, like my own,
But frost nips early in Edinburgh:
Romance-rhythms snap and harden
At the first night-touch, and a Comeley Bank garden
Lies ghastly at dawn, ransacked, root-strewn,
Torn by Carlyle's wild hands in the uprush
Of despair: fumbling amiss for the bride's blush,
They had found only ice of her.

Overweight of grim bludgeoning thought
Crushed the light skill of love-grace:
Fierce volcanic tongues smouldered there,
High in the skull, poised for the public ear.
The seer, inept on levels where senses brought
Vision in pure pleasure, in storm-rite
Rapture between two alone, set the blight
Worming towards farm-clods and Cheyne Walk base.

John Knox in Edinburgh bred children,
Found bride-bloom sweet, yet he could preach
Stone-hard as Jane's husband, wedded to truth's cause;
But the Knox-core gaped empty, wrenched by ego claws,
In this savage doubting Thomas, whose bitten
Soul raged for mastery through the mind's grind,
The hectoring intellect, the unit self-refined,
Blocking communion, forcing a breach.

I grew in these men's shades, and never
Lost the Comeley Bank lesson: I would not wed
The thundering brain-cloud or art's dream-guise.
I ventured brideward with prayer and heart-ties
Shaping my needs as a believer;
And though I wed in autumn I wrung no root
From a frosty earth, but embraced the absolute
Crag-tongue of Christ and a joy bedded.

# Wessex and Lyonnesse

An hour before I stood on Bulbarrow
I watched the hermit Powys, ruddy and leonine,
Puff pipe-smoke musingly
Into a modest book-strewn room.
He had just soaked bread-and-butter in his tea,
Explaining that Jesus did
Something like that. But there was no Judas, no
Croak of fate's craft in the Dorset valley.
As I waved farewell through the clear notching sunshine
The Hardy-refuting peace was solid.

I felt exultant on the massive green brow
With High Stoy in haze, the bland Stour winding seaward
Through late summer's restful flourish of trees;
Yet I gleaned no hint of the true cause,
The destined link with my half-breathed romantic vow.

The breeze brought no quiver across Egdon
From a young heart labouring hiddenly
Down there beside the calm Channel —
Heart bruised by a knuckle of false tide
At the end of a cramped, pious tunnel.
Already, though unknown to me,
Her eyes were questioning the quiet palms
And the white chipped anvil, the Isle of Slingers,
Seeking, beyond ascetic laws,
Love's reborn shape that no iron cuts or hammers.

I soon turned back, reluctantly,
To a savage Cornwall — scoop's bite, earth-rind peeling,
Crashing in fetid lumps during night shifts,
Purged at pit-level or on a kiln-pan.
But a radiance stayed, played on the lanced and reeling
Loam: I was strangely mature, having lost all dark belief
In the chronic martyrdom of man.

I denied pit-torture, she the dusty prison,
For eighteen years more. . . .
Now she prepares the hallowed meal
In a so-called hermit's modest book-strewn room
Down in Hardy's Lyonnesse.
But there is no sop, no Judas,
No croak of Fates or chorus of the Pities;
Only solid peace, out-pacing the martyr-season.

# The Frosted Image

Crude designs are mildewed on a huddle of walls,
Explored by vermin and cynical snails
In the dark hours when the unripe dreamer
Is jarred by an adjoining growl of mature heat;
And high above them sometimes space-men soar,
Moon-bound, sleeping in turns as they mount,
Smiling at the obsolete slum child,
The bud of gunman and whore,
Far back, surely frosted,
Down there on the advanced planet.

In my own cramped room I have said
That a true vision flowers undaunted
By rats' reek and sodden paper.
I have pointed to Bernadette
Racing to her Lady, blithe in the dawn-flare,
Retrieved from the motions on the straw bed
And the lice clotting her hair.

But the saint's view is rare, seeming of small account
When men circle so high to bestride
Dead space where open breath is denied —
Science shedding an astral glamour
That mocks the clammy sore, the laggard place
Where design and breeding breath lack space.

# A Mother's Tragedy

(M.A.P.: Easter 1973)

On ancient hills a frightening rift
Expanded to her grieving eyes,
Swallowed her quest.
The inner silence, grim and stoned,
Emptied her will of every taste.

Her son's eclipse, the tolling doubt
Renewed, recast as tongueless bell,
Robbed the calm plot.
The lost face pierced a wincing moon;
It breathed and cried and would not set.

Tenacious love, burdened too long
With miming shifts of mood and plea,
Tapped the dazed lip.
Her worn feet quavered in false lights;
The bell swung mute on time's mishap.

Behind the pillowed mask, behind
The cipher and the crack of fate,
We bid God watch
The tillage of the unscathed folds
Her stars once blessed, her woes now teach.

# Whispers

These whispers must come from ahead,
From a point where the road bends round
Into faith-flushed terrain again,
Beyond the last factory-shed
Of secular mirage. They have haunted
Not merely my raw birth-dower
Of iron tracks, quarry-faces
And thin sand-scratching furze,
But palm and pebbly beach more fitly hers
Whose whisper warms, confirms their message.

To tire of current babble
Could not evoke such clear intimations
Unless something lived and moved, articulate
Outside the jarring circuit: without this,
My fret or boredom could bring only
The screwed frost of silence.

I am not tired: the whispers give me power,
Not insulating, sealing me in an archaic climate.
I have trudged the menaced and changeful way
Down through the twentieth century,
Smelt petrol, drugs and bleaching chemicals,
Passed super-markets, laboratories, clinics.

I have heard men's voices barking on the moon,
Bomb-clouts and the shrieked pop tune;
Stood under excavators that baptized me
With rain from their poised dull teeth;
Seen white spoil-heaps, first conical, turn oblong,
And subtler crusts of thought turn sour.

I know what today's paper claims
For the birth pill, what some bishops preach
About a shrivelled God and shrivelling morals,
And what young trendy poets write
Concerning urinals.
I have caught the dry jargon, watched the expert hands
Plaster neat labels on holy places,
Call the terrible secret of God a neurosis,
The terrible insights of sex an obsession.

The whispers that echo in my lines
Laugh gently among buds of the future,
For a wind will rise against the vulgar term,
And terror is truth in the intermediate
Regions between nullity and centre.

If flawed cells flared in the murmuring germ
Till I rasped and hurled rocks like a clay titan,
There is no regret on the lulled levels,
For they are private. The rebel's
Fire and peril remain; intense
Listening stiffens my rejection
Of the broad escape-route's signs.
Even her pebbly beach under the calm bran-
Coloured cliff borders the oolite quarries
Where stone was cracked to bear
A whispering gallery, like our faith's, ringed by nightmare.

# Herman Melville

I searched through white death native
  And coloured life not native but showered
Amid the strange torments of my voyages
  Where thought-shells melted, vision grew
                                    blood-powered.

Coral and coconut and glittering dance —
  A hint of undraped priestliness, of Eden;
But I saw girls' naked brown breasts gnawed
  By the ulcerous lips of our whalemen.

A sewn shroud on the *Acushnet's* deck
  Under the spume-flogged, venomous masts:
I felt a sea-monster heave at the hull;
  Within nature's storm, the unknown counterblasts.

Ultimate claimed a voice in me,
  In the obscure hunt and haunting:
I would see Christ's white tomb, sense Ahab's white whale
  Rise, bulk and vapour writhing.

From soft lagoons of the Marquesas,
  Where traders bring plague and our priests barrenly bow,
I brought a cry of seed and selfhood,
  Hurled at some force that shrouds my genius now.

Huge floundering rhythms came — no neat art,
  No nimble song on a harboured rigging:
My deeps, born dour as Ben Nevis,
  Were split by a mystic deluging.

I was husband and father, yet I echoed
    Whale-spout and archangel's horn.
Harpoons may still drift where my Southern saga
    Closed: I bled then from America's scorn.

That dark demented clash in remote waters
    Faded in cold ambiguity:
Would Christ slay pride of doubt or pride of faith
    Or pride of blood, or save, transform all three?

No clue, no settlement: the hideous wrangle
    Hardens the world. But I have withdrawn:
My wife the true surrendered island,
    The sole, frail hint of palm and throne.

# St Gildas

(In tribute to Alexis Carrel)

Albatross, petrel, or a more fabulous bird
Might fitly watch him while he stands alone
On the shrunken cliff, that ageing, puzzling Carrel —
Monk-like and surgical,
Wrestling and detached, cautious and love-spurred.
The last splintered ardours of sunset
Sag past him to soften the mainland coast.

He scans the worn gaunt bones of his island home
And the dividing tide racing more swiftly,
Grinding louder as the night nears.
Fearlessly his mind and spirit
Probe on, knitting tissues of the unknown.

If weird bleak Brittany
Has Celtic ties with Cornwall, I care little.
Such roots are brief, twin stems of tongue and custom
Break on petty ground. No place can touch me
Until I know a great soul touched it,
Was torn, reborn there, threw on rock and tree,
On street or meadow-scene,
Some clue to the heaven-sowing presence,
    some sign of exit
From an untravailling routine.

I look towards St Gildas
Merely to honour a soul scarred and lonely —
This scientist and mystic, weaver of extremes,
Who trusts the curt rational data
And the flaming creed, reveres both chart and chant.

As he notes the imprisoned, moon-swayed toil of the sea
He recalls the Lourdes pools, stirred by the free,
   immaculate
Virtue of an unmapped star.
The open, unchilled truth is less distant,
Though the known cliff is cramped and crumbling.

Methods. Voices in the wind.
Dissect.    Anoint.
The clash first, then the homeward fusion-point.

# Wamba Convent 1964

Rebel soldiers! Oh Mary, here's Congo hell's
Heat, denser than we dreamed, inside the cloisters.
Brothel-glint, war custom, burst on our cells;
The scars of black tusks deface the ivory
When veil and habit are torn from us.
*Turris eburnea,*
*Ora pro nobis.*

Never again like your earthly body, gracious
Virgin unstained, will our once nun-null
Woman-forms curve and tremble at the Cross:
Towers we sealed for our shielding Bridegroom
Brute-shadows loot, quenching the candled kiss.
*Turris eburnea,*
*Ora pro nobis.*

Did you speak comfort through the English prisoner,
Not of our fold, wearing no crucifix,
But sharing our shame? She claimed, Mother,
No assault can spoil, soil Christ's bridal temple,
That more than soul stays pure in this abyss.
*Turris eburnea,*
*Ora pro nobis.*

True, there's no traffic here, no flesh-fire's
Sold or exchanged: perhaps the limb-locking vow
Need quail no more at rape than at death-virus.
A body Christ bought, mine, still whole?
Could spirit but show
Links, overlappings, where its real robe is!
*Turris eburnea,*
*Ora pro nobis.*

We came coifed against Congo's drumming arts,
Built our base, God's hidden forge in the forest.
How far the armour, the mystic woman-parts,
Cover us now is His secret, guessed
Dimly through anguish of involved senses.
*Turris eburnea,*
*Ora pro nobis.*

# A Clash at Ikpe

(An incident in the life of Mary Slessor)

God palaver bad for seed,
Say the Egbo drums, bouncing outside the mud church.
There's a night service, an old Scots spinster
Praying, crooning hymns, naming a clean law
In the swamp-sour jungle village.

Black youth asserts its lush, defiant splendour,
Bold with the heavy soil, the roof of wet leaves,
And the couching leopards.
Naked bodies catch drum-rhythm, writhe and sweat
In the light of wagging torches, in the clawing fire-glow
That glints on gin bottles drained at hut doors.
Couples stamp to the offer and orgy
With lips wrenched, gross and slobbering:
Human hyena laughter, smothered
In dung-dressed hair or hot greasy flesh,
Cackles against the chaste hymn.

The missioner, grim-faced but undeterred,
Carries the service through, ends with thanksgiving.
Pale thought and prime rules
Have wrapped a time-bomb of Galilee's grace
Dropped on the blood-raw, fleering fetishes,
Witchmen's dabbling, worship of phallus and skull,
Dread of poisonous *juju*, curse of the tree-god, M'biam.

Not so remote either, this crude clash,
From the West's way now, my way once
When my wet clay, fertile with weeds and waving
Plumes of heresy, instinct-growths,
Felt the slap of the harmattan — dust-storms,
Church-bred, choking the ego's
(Low as Egbo's) creative thrust,
Shrivelling, driving it back
To the wind's own desert source for rebirth.

Now, with the medieval romance discarded,
The Reformation fusion (dogma
And sense-joy in marriage) ignored,
What Western artist, poet, lover,
Does not stage somewhere a private Ikpe,
Revolt against the saints' desert,
The truth that's myth-like until it stings?
Seed lapsed, adulterated, bad for the Word,
Having lost the old ways of atonement,
Needs the snapping dust, the explosion among the fruit.

# Affirmative Way

Razored by frost and thaw, a quarry rim
Collapsed one night, quite near my home.
A curved jut of spongy topsoil,
Heavy with bush-clumps and a stone hedge,
Was slowly loosened, severed, poised
In a brief tremor of roots and boulders,
Then thundering, a horror of rock-splinters,
Earth-clots and mangled twigs, into the
   moon-fingered pit,
Taking half the road with it.

I looked next day at the gashed ground,
Sheer drop from the road's centre,
And at the deep zigzag cracks
Networked for yards around.
I felt baulked, deprived, as this road led
To the ridge of downs, my favourite spot
For mystic musings at twilight.

I recalled the maxims of the negative school,
The trite line of condolence:
'The blind glimpse truths that sighted people miss;
The deaf hear subtler tongues astir within;
The paralysed thrill with a rarer bliss. . . .'
None of that patter here! I could see
What became of my only highway
When a quarry-face caved in.

The soul's road to divine wisdom
Passes so close to the sensuous quarry
That a maiming of the fertile ledge —
Loss of touch, sound, movement, colour,
Topple of beauty's thrust and chafe —

Tears half the road away,
Leaving the rest unsafe.

You cannot trust an intuition
Flashed merely as a compensation.
The insight, the forced dream,
The theory, which a cripple shapes
To train, sustain, explain himself,
Falls sterile and untested,
Making no bridge for brisk feet
Blundering where herd-perils teem.

'The diviner learns because he lacks,'
Say the glib pundits. Well, take the extreme —
Abelard's curb, the pale scar,
The hollow voice on the broken path.
Did the eunuch match a Luther's fiery vision,
A Patmore's delicate victory of grace?
Not for *them* a passion's cold aftermath.

I can trust only the intact road
Marking the pure unmutilated edge
Before the frost came, before the quarry-crust fell.
My creed was proved by keen sense-evidence —
Tossed tint, girlhood's frown and smile,
Bold scarps crossed by lusty horses;
And I still ignore the blockage, hearing
The old winds move above the riper seed-swell.

# On the Burial of a Poet Laureate

(To C.D.L.: May 1972)

Laureate, your heart rests, after a rainy Whitsun,
    Close to grave Hardy's heart which bore
Much the same toils: warrant of Western sunset,
The church towers fading, the unransomed moor
Thrusting the outcasts, stoic or Promethean,
    To sea's verge and poet's core.

You thrilled the psalm until the bells turned bitter
    On your sharp, copious mind:
Climate of revolution, honest thinking,
Shrivelled for you the long solace of mankind.
No mystic, you sought a basis newer, fitter,
    Down to the common grind.

You scanned the pylon, the bold tractor lurching,
    The bomb-gash on the town,
Found fuel awhile among the plotting comrades;
But there came storm and flight, with Red rhythms blown,
Silenced by Devon's thick dialect of suffering:
    Your spirit then groped alone.

I could join you there, in the discovery
    That the resinous craft,
Pure form, needs inward friction, the soul bowed, searching
For truths unchanged by sunset: not the draught
Or drive of mundane systems, but a crosstree,
    Grail-blood, the cosmic graft.

You told me once my firm and clarion metres
    Suspended your disbelief:
So rebel-rough, incisive, free from mildew
Was the faith  erupting in me after brief
Tensions of darkness: you saw the mournful fetters
    Burst on my clay-pit reef.

What changed the climate on my gritty island,
    Kept me from faith's decline?
Two hearts, bereft and yearning, make Dorset soil
Nobler now and strangely nearer mine;
But rainless Whitsun nourishes my clay-land
    With an undimmed altar-sign.

# Royal Wedding

Sun sparkles on London crowds, though here in the west
November fog sneaks round the dying shrub-stems
Outside one of England's humblest cottages:
A century old, blunt granite, and industrial rubble
Fumbling close by, with some garages.
We who live wedded here
Sit cleansed by Abbey music, fanfare,
And solemn voices flowing at the crest
Of another dream-drive among regal gems.

This is no hollow pomp, this is root and haven,
The sane oasis where hearts pause and listen
To the intoning tongue of half-forgotten springs,
The deep historic soundings
From the rock-base, at the courtly arrival.

Feel now, how mean and small
Is the modern desert, drably efficient,
Swept by sullen agitation
Where the grey waste meets the red sand!
We have feared the ignoble trampling
Set as tomorrow's march for our people;
The alien expanse with no gracious order,
No traditional command,
But only the raw rasp of gravelly bluster
And machine-geared instinct, blind through separation
From the silken splendour of a reverent vow.

Bones of great lovers lie in this oasis:
Browning and Tennyson, who showed
    what the English meant
By marriage: rose-flush in a hushed garden,
Sheath of oak-shade, massive and wholesome,
Folding the plain vein, a pledge
Of ancient power and knowledge,
Northern and Christian. We need this
Revived, need voices to restore the flow,
Spread the crowned wisdom, let the chanting
Waters redeem the dry furrow.

# A Wife on an Autumn Anniversary

Much to sort out: rending rain on screes,
Sun-strut, prick of mists,
Thunder on tin tabernacles,
Moon-glide on cavern votaries,
And the moralist's
Dilemma between keys and shackles.

But I know the weather and the gate
That called and fitted
The woman I am — love's witness shy
Among your psalming leaves. I can state
When falsehood quitted
And the residue summed our earth and sky.

Decades of treading in shifts of air
That left scorch-print or frostbite
At bolted or gaping entrances.
Few were authentic, though hearts share,
Through flood-terror at night
And noon's stare at ruin, some nakedness.

Not the highest, not this where your leaves veil me
And I trace the true lines back
To sprays of glad weather on a palmy outpost,
My body sensing the upwarped key.
Tin and stone grew black
In storm — love's vision dead almost.

Tragic depth takes a spurious turn,
And the haggard lesson
Must be unlearned in the ripe, safe coupling.
My first desire at the beaded cavern
Matched sun-wooed screes: you won
Against false weather on your sapling.

Five years with your positive bright leaves!
I, too, hear the rumour
Scraped on the autumn vein: we meet
Pain in a new context. Our earth grieves
Within the golden humour
Rayed from soul's heaven's unshifting heat.